God Leads Us Along
Hymns for the Journey

Arranged for Solo Piano by

Jeff Bennett

Editor: Lloyd Larson
Music Engraving: MacMusic, Inc.
Cover Design: Katie Hufford

ISBN: 978-0-7877-1833-6

lillenas
PUBLISHING COMPANY

www.lorenz.com

Foreword

I am always excited to write and create a new collection of piano solos. With these new hymn settings I wanted to arrange several of them in a style differently than what is normally done.

There is a saying: *Life is a journey, not a destination.* Our Christian journey is important, leading us to the ultimate destination of heaven. Many of these hymns are inspired by scripture and, I believe, will aid your journey. I pray you are encouraged spiritually and musically! God bless you!

—*Jeff Bennett*

About the Arranger

Jeff Bennett is one of today's most prolific arrangers for sacred keyboard music with over 700 published arrangements. He was a major contributor to a new worship hymnal and is a respected pianist, arranger, and recording artist with several publishers around the country. He is not only a writer of church music, but has also performed on a recording for Disney and has arranged for artists like the late Marvin Hamlisch. He is the creative mind behind the four-piano recording and concert tour, *A Festival of Keyboards!* His performances have included local churches, college campuses, and concert halls including Carnegie Hall. He has performed on national television as well.

Jeff performs solo concerts throughout the United States and abroad, and leads master classes in arranging and keyboard skills. Visit www.jeffbennettmusic.com for more information. Jeff and his wife, Sarah, have two adult age daughters.

God Leads Us Along
Jeff Bennett

Contents

God Leads Us Along

G. A. YOUNG
Arr. by Jeff Bennett

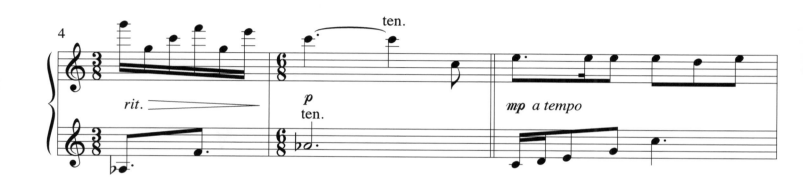

His Eye Is on the Sparrow

CHARLES H. GABRIEL
Arr. by Jeff Bennett

I Need Thee Every Hour

ROBERT LOWRY
Arr. by Jeff Bennett

Since Jesus Came into My Heart

CHARLES H. GABRIEL
Arr. by Jeff Bennett

Nothing but the Blood

ROBERT LOWRY
Arr. by Jeff Bennett

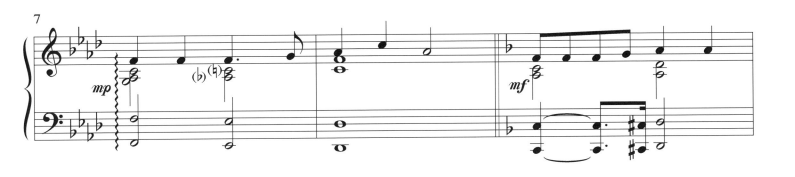

718336-25

God Will Take Care of You

W. STILLMAN MARTIN
Arr. by Jeff Bennett

With steady motion ♩ = ca. 112

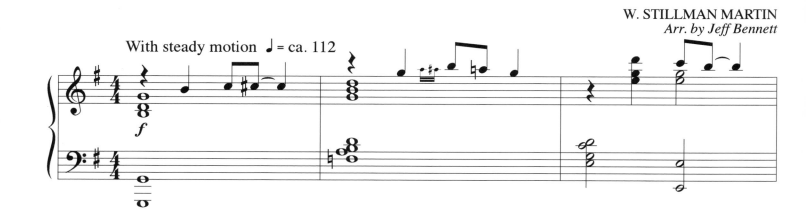

'Tis So Sweet to Trust in Jesus

A Quiet Meditation

WILLIAM J. KIRKPATRICK
Arr. by Jeff Bennett

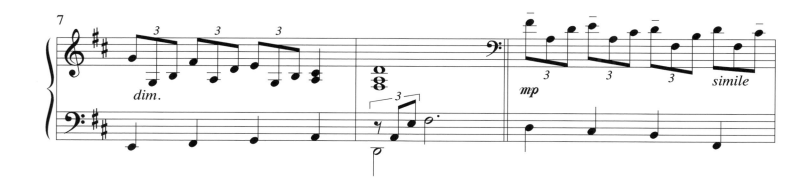

Do Not
Photocopy

Amazing Grace

JOHN NEWTON
Arr. by Jeff Bennett

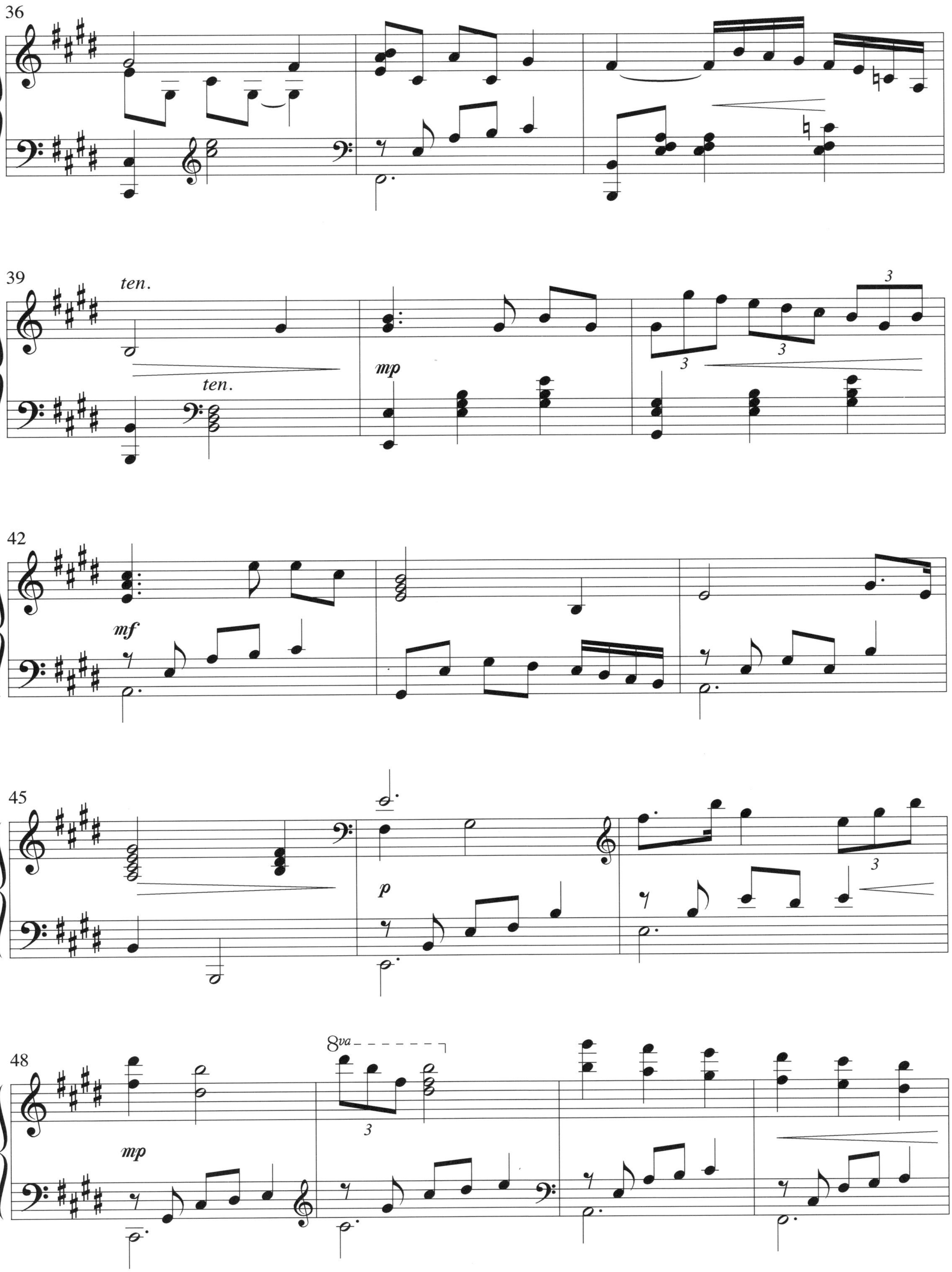
36
39
ten.
ten.
mp
3
42
mf
45
p
3
48
mp
8va
3

Majestically ♩ = ca. 72

Just a Closer Walk with Thee

Anonymous
Arr. by Jeff Bennett

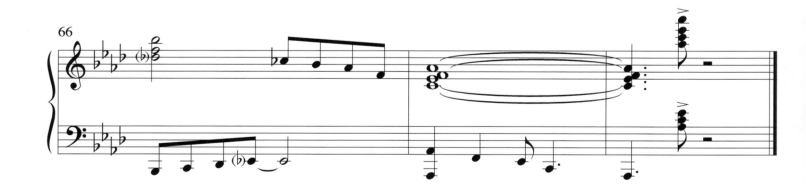

In the Garden

C. AUSTIN MILES
Arr. by Jeff Bennett